Healthy Dog Food Cookbook for Every Owner

Dog Food Recipes to Keep Your Pet Living Longer

By: Angel Burns

© 2019 Angel Burns, All Rights Reserved.

License Notices

This book or parts thereof might not be reproduced in any format for personal or commercial use without the written permission of the author. Possession and distribution of this book by any means without said permission is prohibited by law.

All content is for entertainment purposes and the author accepts no responsibility for any damages, commercially or personally, caused by following the content.

Table of Contents

Healthy Dog Food Recipes 6

    Recipe 1: Cheesy Cookies 7

    Recipe 2: Liver Dinner 9

    Recipe 3: Doggy Meatloaf 11

    Recipe 4: Doggie Chili 13

    Recipe 5: Turkey and Vegetable Dinner 15

    Recipe 6: Sweet Potato Chews 18

    Recipe 7: Vegetable & Turkey Delight 20

    Recipe 8: Almond and Banana Treats 22

    Recipe 9: Chicken Casserole 24

    Recipe 10: Carob Dog Biscuits 26

    Recipe 11: Chicken and Vegetable Medley 29

    Recipe 12: Herb Treats 31

    Recipe 13: Chicken Patty 33

Recipe 14: Gingerbread Treat 35

Recipe 15: Easy Turkey and Rice 37

Recipe 16: Apple Crunch Pupcakes 40

Recipe 17: Fruit Parfait 42

Recipe 18: Beef Stew 44

Recipe 19: Leftovers Trail Mix 48

Recipe 20: Pork & Eggs 50

Recipe 21: Healthy Pumpkin Balls 52

Recipe 22: Crockpot Dog Food 55

Recipe 23: Bacon Peanut Butter Biscuits 57

Recipe 24: Stir Fry Beef Meal 60

Recipe 25: Basic Dog Biscuits 62

Recipe 26: Doggie Meatballs 64

Recipe 27: Frozen Peanut Butter Yogurt Dog Treats ... 67

Recipe 28: Salmon and Spinach 69

Recipe 29: Quinoa Doddie Plate 71

Recipe 30: Easy Chicken Stew 73

About the Author 75

Author's Afterthoughts 77

Healthy Dog Food Recipes

HHHHHHHHHHHHHHHHHHHHHHHHHHHHHHHH

Recipe 1: Cheesy Cookies

The majority of dogs love cheese, but it can become quite difficult to find a cheesy treat that's genuinely healthy for your dog. That's where this recipe comes into play!

Makes: 6

Total Prep Time: 30 mins.

Ingredient List:

- Cheese (½ cup, cheddar, shredded)
- Water (2 tablespoons)
- Vegetable oil (2 tablespoons)
- Egg (1)
- Cornmeal (2 cups)
- Applesauce (½ cup)

HHHHHHHHHHHHHHHHHHHHHHHHHHHHHHHHH

Instructions:

1. Preheat oven to 325 degrees Fahrenheit.

2. Mix all the ingredients in a bowl.

3. Drop the mixture in different shapes or balls on a baking sheet and use a spoon to flatten.

4. Bake for a minimum of 25 minutes.

5. Store and serve as desired.

Recipe 2: Liver Dinner

The majority of dogs enjoy liver-based meals, which makes this both a healthy and tasty meal for your dog.

Makes: 5 cups

Total Prep Time: 20 mins.

Ingredient List:

- Corn (2 cups)
- Olive oil (1 tablespoon)
- Chicken liver (1 lb.)
- Green beans (2 cups, trimmed)
- All-purpose flour (2 tablespoons)

HHHHHHHHHHHHHHHHHHHHHHHHHHHHHHHHH

Instructions:

1. Cut the chicken liver into thin strips and gradually mix with flour.

2. Over medium heat, heat olive oil and add the chicken liver. Cook for a minimum of 2 minutes.

3. Add the green beans and corn. Cover and cook for approximately 7-10 minutes, until the green beans are thoroughly cooked.

4. Don't be startled by the color! Your dog will adore this dish.

5. Serve cooled and place leftovers in the refrigerator but serve warm.

Recipe 3: Doggy Meatloaf

This delicious meatloaf is filled with vegetables and bound with oats that has healthy fiber for your growing pup.

Makes: 5 cups

Total Prep Time: 55 mins.

Ingredient List:

- Pork (½ lb.)
- Ground beef (½ lb.)
- Ricotta cheese (½ cup)
- Egg (1)
- Rolled oats (1 cup)
- Vegetable medley (1 cup, frozen)

HHHHHHHHHHHHHHHHHHHHHHHHHHHHHHHH

Instructions:

1. Preheat oven to 375 degrees Fahrenheit. Lightly grease a meatloaf pan.

2. Mix together ingredients in large bowl.

3. Press mixture into the pan. Bake for approximately 40-50 minutes.

4. Slice and serve once cooled. Refrigerate any leftovers.

Recipe 4: Doggie Chili

In order for your dog to maintain his health and stay active they require huge masses of protein, which they get from whole meat sources, especially where young puppies are concerned. A good sample of protein is fresh chicken. Beans can also provide dogs with a significant amount of protein. Your dog can exceptionally benefit from this recipe, since it is a fresh blend of beans, chicken and vegetables which he'll surely enjoy because it's delicious.

Makes: 8 cups

Total Prep Time: 15 mins.

Ingredient List:

- Chicken breasts (4)
- Carrots (1 cup, diced)
- Chicken broth (4 cups, unsalted)
- Kidney beans (1 cup, drained)
- Tomato paste (½ cup)
- Beans (1 cup, black, drained)

HHHHHHHHHHHHHHHHHHHHHHHHHHHHHHHHH

Instructions:

1. Remove excess fat from chicken breasts and dice into nickel-sized pieces.

2. Use non-stick skillet to cook chicken breasts, removing when no longer pink.

3. Combine carrots, chicken broth, chicken, and tomato paste in large pot and heat over medium heat. Let cook for about 10 minutes.

4. Let mixture cool and serve.

The leftover chili can feed your dog for up to five days. You can also add ½ tablespoon fish oil to the chili, which will result in good, strong flavors that your dog will love.

Recipe 5: Turkey and Vegetable Dinner

Turkey provides your dog with a wide range of protein while the vegetables contain minerals and some additional vitamins. This recipe is made especially for puppies in need of losing some pounds, this is due to the fact that it contains less fat when compared to the dog dishes made with beef.

Makes: 10 cups

Total Prep Time: 30 mins

Ingredient List:

- Ground turkey (1 lb.)
- Water (4 cups)
- Carrots (1 cup, chopped)
- Fish oil (1 tablespoon, optional)
- Rice (2 cups, brown)
- Beans (1 cup, green, chopped)

HHHHHHHHHHHHHHHHHHHHHHHHHHHHHHHH

Instructions:

1. Over medium heat, preheat a non-stick skillet and add the ground turkey. Cook until the turkey becomes no longer pink then set aside.

2. Over medium high heat add brown rice, turkey and water to a large pot and bring to a boil.

3. Turn down the heat to medium and let the mixture cook for another 13-15 minutes or until the rice has become tender and soft.

4. Add the carrots and green beans to the mixture and cook another 6-10 minutes or until the vegetables are tender.

5. Let cool and serve to your dog.

Note: Leftovers can be stored up to five days in the refrigerator. Avoid using heavy oils when preparing this recipe because they contain a high fat content that may upset your dog's stomach.

Recipe 6: Sweet Potato Chews

This is a really simple recipe with only one ingredient: sweet potato.

Makes: 12

Total Prep Time: 8 hrs.

Ingredient List:

- Sweet potatoes (4)

HHHHHHHHHHHHHHHHHHHHHHHHHHHHHHHHH

Instructions:

1. Thoroughly wash the sweet potatoes before peeling them.

2. Slice into ¼ inch slices (you can achieve this by cutting down the middle which should act as their length).

3. Set dehydrator to approximately 145-155 degrees Fahrenheit, which is usually the max, and leave at that distinct temperature until the slices are completely dried. This will take a minimum of 6-8 hours in order to give slices a chewy texture.

4. If you prefer the treat to be crunchier, extend the period of dehydration until you achieve the desired texture.

Recipe 7: Vegetable & Turkey Delight

Most people usually tend to think of turkey when they are thinking of Thanksgiving, but you'll realize that your beloved dog adores turkey, which will provide him with the nutritional value of protein he needs without a lot of fat. With the addition of rice and a few other vegetables you'll have a nutritious, complete dish ready and waiting for your dog to eat.

Makes: 8 cups

Total Prep Time: 15 mins

Ingredient List:

- Rice (1 cup, brown)
- Water (2 cups)
- Pear (1, diced)
- Broccoli (1 cup, florets)
- Kale (1 cup, chopped)
- Carrots (1 cup, diced)
- Cheese (1 cup, cottage)
- Vegetable oil (3 tablespoons)

HHHHHHHHHHHHHHHHHHHHHHHHHHHHHHHHHHH

Instructions:

1. Cook the rice on your stove and put aside.

2. Add vegetable oil and turkey in a skillet and stir. Add the vegetables, with the exception of the kale, ensuring not to overcook either the vegetables or meat.

3. Add kale and pear.

4. Combine cooked rice and cook for 5 minutes longer.

5. Place in a bowl and add the cottage cheese and mix well.

6. Refrigerate until his next meal.

Recipe 8: Almond and Banana Treats

Dogs enjoy the taste of almonds almost as much as they love the taste of peanut butter, making this a really tasty treat.

Makes: 6

Total Prep Time: 20 mins.

Ingredient List:

- Cinnamon (1 teaspoon, ground)
- Banana (½ of banana)
- Almond Butter (¾ cup, unsalted)
- Egg (1)

HHHHHHHHHHHHHHHHHHHHHHHHHHHHHHHH

Instructions:

1. Preheat oven to 350 degrees Fahrenheit. Use parchment paper to line a baking sheet.

2. In a bowl mash the banana and add the rest of ingredients.

3. Blend well and spoon onto the parchment paper.

4. Bake for a minimum of 10 minutes.

5. Let cool before serving.

Recipe 9: Chicken Casserole

Chicken provides your beloved dog with a great amount of protein which is needed for your dog's development and growth and the vegetables help to give additional flavor to the meal. This meal is highly recommended for your dog because the vegetables will help to improve and allow your dog to have a healthy intestinal tract, while the green beans are needed for making your dog feel full.

Makes: 7 cups

Total Prep Time: 20 mins.

Ingredient List:

- Chicken breasts (4)
- Carrots (½ cup, chopped)
- Oats (½ cup, rolled)
- Beans (½ cup, green, chopped)
- Chicken broth (4 cups, unsalted)
- Broccoli (½ cup, chopped)

HHHHHHHHHHHHHHHHHHHHHHHHHHHHHHHHH

Instructions:

1. Remove the excess amount of fat from chicken breasts before cutting them into small chunks.

2. Over medium heat, heat a non-stick skillet and cook chicken breasts until they are no longer pink.

3. In a large pot, place chicken broth, vegetables and chicken and bring to boil. Let simmer for about 12-15 minutes or until the carrots have become tender.

4. Let cool before serving.

Note: The leftover portion can be refrigerated up to five days, if the chicken breasts become stuck to the skillet, try frying in a small amount of olive oil.

Recipe 10: Carob Dog Biscuits

Carob chips are a good substitute for actual chocolate. Chocolate is bad for dogs and could possibly kill them, but carob is fine. It's important to clarify that these biscuits are not dipped in chocolate to those you share the recipe with.

Makes: 6

Total Prep Time: 35 mins.

Ingredient List:

- Coconut Flour (2 cups)
- Coconut Oil (1 tablespoon)
- Peanut Butter (1 cup, smooth)
- Carob Chips (½ cup, melted)
- Coconut milk (1 cup)
- Maple syrup (1 tablespoon)
- Baking powder (1 teaspoon)
- Baking soda (½ teaspoons)

HHHHHHHHHHHHHHHHHHHHHHHHHHHHHHHHH

Instructions:

1. Preheat oven to 350 degrees Fahrenheit.

2. Combine the baking soda, flour and baking powder in a bowl.

3. Combine the peanut butter, maple syrup and coconut milk in another bowl.

4. Blend both mixtures together and drop by a spoonful onto a baking sheet.

5. Bake for approximately 25 minutes and let cool.

6. In a saucepan melt the carob chips and coconut oil.

7. Let the carob chips mixture cool. Dip the biscuits into mixture.

8. Serve the biscuits after they've cooled.

Recipe 11: Chicken and Vegetable Medley

Dogs just adore chicken as much as they enjoy beef, and your dog will surely love this low-fat meal.

Makes: 6 cups

Total Prep Time: 15 mins.

Ingredient List:

- Chicken breasts (3, cubed)
- Egg (1)
- Vegetable medley (2 cups, frozen)
- Rice (2 cups, brown, cooked)
- Olive oil (1 tablespoon)
- Parsley (3 tablespoons, chopped)

HHHHHHHHHHHHHHHHHHHHHHHHHHHHHHHHHH

Instructions:

1. In a large skillet, heat olive oil over the medium heat. Add the chicken and then cook for a minimum of 5 minutes.

2. Add the brown rice and vegetable medley. Cook for approximately 8-10 minutes, thoroughly mixing.

3. Add in the parsley, gently mixing and remove from heat.

4. Let cool completely before serving. Place any leftovers in the Refrigerator.

Recipe 12: Herb Treats

This is a delicious, crunchy treat enriched and flavored with herbs this is great for both your dog's digestive system and teeth.

Makes: 6

Total Prep Time: 40 mins.

Ingredient List:

- Vegetable oil (1 tablespoon)
- Mint (3 tablespoons, chopped)
- Parsley (3 tablespoons, chopped)
- Flour (2 cups, self-rising)
- Egg (1)
- Honey (1 tablespoon, raw)

HHHHHHHHHHHHHHHHHHHHHHHHHHHHHHHHH

Instructions:

1. Preheat oven to 350 degrees Fahrenheit.

2. In a large bowl mix together the vegetable oil, parsley and mint.

3. Add the flour, honey and egg, thoroughly combine to form a dough. If needed you can add a little water.

4. Form into cookie shapes and bake for approximately 30 minutes

5. Let cool before serving.

Recipe 13: Chicken Patty

This recipe is more similar to a cake than a patty, but it makes your delicious chicken anything but plain and boring. If you prefer you can use turkey.

Makes: 7 cups

Total Prep Time: 45 mins.

Ingredient List:

- Apple (½ cup, diced)
- Carrots (1 cup, diced)
- Kernels (1 cup, corn)
- Rice (2 cups, white, cooked)
- Egg (1)
- Chicken (1 lb., ground)

HHHHHHHHHHHHHHHHHHHHHHHHHHHHHHHH

Instructions:

1. Heat oven to 350 degrees Fahrenheit.

2. Mix chicken, carrots and corn in a large bowl.

3. Add white rice, egg and apple mixing well.

4. Press into a baking dish. Bake for a minimum of 36-40 minutes.

5. Slice and serve once cooled. Place any leftovers in the refrigerator.

Recipe 14: Gingerbread Treat

Ginger is the perfect way to bring life and flavor to your dog's treat, making this the ideal recipe.

Makes: 6

Total Prep Time: 30 mins.

Ingredient List:

- Flour (6 oz, self-rising)
- Peanut butter (3 oz)
- Water (4 tablespoons, hot)
- Cinnamon (½ teaspoons, ground)
- Ginger (2 teaspoons, ground)

HHHHHHHHHHHHHHHHHHHHHHHHHHHHHHHH

Instructions:

1. Preheat oven to 350 degrees Fahrenheit.

2. In a bowl mix the peanut butter and hot water, stirring well.

3. Add the ginger, cinnamon and flour, mix until a dough has formed. If needed you may need to add a little more water.

4. Use hands to knead dough before flattening to ¼ inch thickness. Cut as desired.

5. Bake for approximately 15-20 minutes and let cool before serving.

Recipe 15: Easy Turkey and Rice

Your dog will praise you for this healthy, nutritious and scrumptious meal; he'll gobble it right up.

Makes: 8 cups

Total Prep Time: 15 mins.

Ingredient List:

- Rice (1 ½ cups)
- Olive oil (1 tablespoon)
- Turkey (3 lbs., ground)
- Spinach (3 cups, finely chopped)
- Carrots (2 large, shredded)
- Zucchini (1 medium, shredded)
- Peas (½ cup, frozen)
- Chicken broth (½ cup, unsalted)

HHHHHHHHHHHHHHHHHHHHHHHHHHHHHHHHHH

Instructions:

1. In a large pot cook the rice according to the instructions given on the package and set aside.

2. Over medium heat, heat oil in a large pot and add the ground turkey or chicken.

Cook fully until it becomes or looks almost dry.

3. Separate the ground meat into small pieces as it cooks to avoid large lumps.

4. Add the spinach, zucchini, carrots, and peas.

5. Add the broth and cook until fluid has almost evaporated and vegetables are ready and fully cooked, approximately 10 minutes.

6. Add the rice and thoroughly mix. Let cool completely before serving.

Recipe 16: Apple Crunch Pupcakes

Your pup will enjoy these delectable mini cupcakes designed to attracted just about any hungry puppy.

Makes: 6

Total Prep Time: 1 hr. 30 mins.

Ingredient List:

- Vanilla extract (¼ teaspoons)
- Applesauce (¼ cup, unsweetened)
- Flour (4 cups, whole wheat)
- Apple chips (1 cup, unsweetened and dried)
- Honey (2 tablespoons)
- Egg (1 medium)
- Water (2 ¾ cups)
- Baking powder (1 tablespoon)

HHHHHHHHHHHHHHHHHHHHHHHHHHHHHHHHHH

Instructions:

1. Preheat oven to 350 degrees Fahrenheit.

2. Mix the honey, water, vanilla and applesauce in bowl. Add the remaining ingredients and gradually mix until well-blended.

3. Grease muffin pans lightly and pour the mixture inside.

4. Let bake for approximately 1 hour until toothpick placed in the center comes out completely clean.

Recipe 17: Fruit Parfait

It's a good practice to treat your dog to a dessert once in a while. This Fruit parfait is a combination of dairy products and fruit. Your pup will love the great flavor of this fruit parfait and will also benefit from the protein and vitamins it contains.

Makes: 6

Total Prep Time: 45 mins.

Ingredient List:

- Yogurt (½ cup, non-fat)
- Applesauce (½ cup)
- Strawberries (½ cup, diced)
- Blueberries (½ cup, diced)

HHHHHHHHHHHHHHHHHHHHHHHHHHHHHHHHH

Instructions:

1. Mix together all the ingredients in a medium-sized bowl. Ensure that the fruit is well-blended and the yogurt is smooth.

2. Serve to your dog in small portions.

Note: This fruit parfait due to the contents can only be stored in the fridge for up to seven days. This mixture is considerably heavy, so it's advised that you reduce the quantity of the food you regularly give your dog when he is fed the fruit parfait.

Recipe 18: Beef Stew

This recipe is essentially a variant of the beef stew that we humans eat but some modifications have been made to suit dogs. The recipe consists of fresh vegetables for essential vitamins, meat for protein, and gravy for an additional flavor. This recipe is a good substitute for wet, commercial dog foods.

Makes: 5 cups

Total Prep Time: 35 mins.

Ingredient List:

- Sweet Potato (1 small)
- Flour (½ cup)
- Beef (1 lb., stewing)
- Carrots (½ cup, diced)
- Green beans (½ cup, diced)
- Vegetable oil (1 tablespoon)
- Water (½ cup)

HHHHHHHHHHHHHHHHHHHHHHHHHHHHHHHHH

Instructions:

1. Place the sweet potato into the microwave and let cook for approximately 7-8 minutes, until it becomes tender but firm. Remove and set aside.

2. Slice the stewing beef into smaller chunks (nickel sized). Use vegetable oil (1 tablespoon) to cook stewing beef for a minimum of 15 minutes over medium heat.

3. Ensure beef chunks are cooked properly before removing them from the pan.

4. Reserve drippings and dice the sweet potato.

5. Place the drippings over medium-low heat and Gradually add the flour and water. Continue whisking until a thick gravy forms.

6. Add the green beans, carrots, sweet potato, and the meat to gravy and gradually stir until coated.

7. Continue this process for about 8-10 minutes to allow the carrots to become tender.

6. Let cool and serve.

Note: You can refrigerate the extra stew and serve to your dog at a later time. Instead of preparing the gravy yourself, here's a convenient tip, purchase the gravy from your local food stores.

Recipe 19: Leftovers Trail Mix

Leftovers can be used to make a great trail mix for your dog. Just look for these ingredients in your fridge to make a tasty mix which can act as a snack for your dog, or to pack up if you're going for a hike.

Makes: 1 bowl

Total Prep Time: 20 mins.

Ingredient List:

- Vegetables (no onions)
- Pieces of meat (remove flavoring if meat is seasoned)
- Fruit (no raisins or grapes)
- Potatoes

HHHHHHHHHHHHHHHHHHHHHHHHHHHHHHHHH

Instructions:

1. Cut all the ingredients into ½ inch pieces.

2. Use cooking spray to spray the ingredients.

3. Place the ingredients in a food dehydrator. Alternatively, preheat oven to 200 degrees Fahrenheit and bake until the mix is dry.

Recipe 20: Pork & Eggs

You'll find that this recipe heavily protein based, devoid of anything at all that could cause your dog's bad cholesterol to rise.

Makes: 6 cups

Total Prep Time: 30 mins.

Ingredient List:

- Bread (2 slices, white)
- Pork (¼ lb., ground)
- Eggs (2, hard boiled)
- Rice (2 cups, white)

HHHHHHHHHHHHHHHHHHHHHHHHHHHHHHHHH

Instructions:

1. Ensure eggs are properly cooked before chopping them.

2. Cook the ground pork, draining away any excessive fat.

3. Place the pork with your eggs and cook the rice like you would normally do.

4. Chop bread, removing the crust.

5. Add the bread to the egg and pork mixture.

6. Combine all the ingredients and serve. Make sure that you store any leftovers in the refrigerator.

Recipe 21: Healthy Pumpkin Balls

These pumpkin balls are great treats for your dog, not only because they're delicious but also because they are rich in vitamin A, iron, fiber, potassium, and beta-carotene.

Makes: 8

Total Prep Time: 30 mins.

Ingredient List:

- Vegetable oil (2 tablespoons)
- Baking powder (¼ teaspoons)
- Molasses (4 tablespoons)
- Cinnamon (1 teaspoon, optional)
- Flour (2 cups, whole wheat)
- Water (4 tablespoons)
- Baking soda (¼ teaspoons)
- Pumpkin (½ cup, canned)

HHHHHHHHHHHHHHHHHHHHHHHHHHHHHHHHH

Instructions:

1. Preheat the oven to 350 degrees Fahrenheit.

2. Mix the vegetable oil, molasses, pumpkin and water in a bowl. Add the baking soda, wheat flour, cinnamon and baking powder and gradually stir until the dough becomes soft.

3. Take small spoonfuls of dough and use your hands to roll into balls. It is advised that you wet your hands first for a better form.

4. Grease a cookie sheet lightly and place the balls on it. Use a fork to flatten.

5. Let the pumpkin balls bake for a minimum of 25 minutes until they become hard.

Recipe 22: Crockpot Dog Food

In some cases, you just want to provide your dog with the finest you can offer, but you unfortunately don't have the time to cook a meal that is both tasty and healthy. This is where this slow cooker dish comes into play.

Makes: 12 cups

Total Prep Time: 5 hours

Ingredient List:

- Zucchini (1 cup, chopped)
- Broccoli (1 cup, florets)
- Water (4 cups)
- Quinoa (1 cup)
- Ground beef (2 lb., lean)
- Kidney beans (1 can, rinsed)

HHHHHHHHHHHHHHHHHHHHHHHHHHHHHHHHHH

Instructions:

1. Place all the ingredients in a crockpot. On low heat cook for a minimum of 5 hours.

2. Stir the pot to thoroughly mix everything well.

3. Let cool and serve. Refrigerate any leftovers.

Recipe 23: Bacon Peanut Butter Biscuits

Peanut butter and bacon are most dog's favorite treat / snack. Your dog will be left craving for more of these biscuits.

Ingredient List:

- Peanut butter (1 cup, creamy, unsalted)
- Milk (¾ cup)
- Egg (1)
- Flour (2 cups whole wheat)
- Oats (⅓ cup rolled)
- Bacon (3 strips, cooked, chopped)

HHHHHHHHHHHHHHHHHHHHHHHHHHHHHHHHHHHH

Instructions:

1. Preheat oven to 325 degrees Fahrenheit. Grease cookie sheet lightly.

2. Combine the peanut butter, oats, milk, egg and bacon in a bowl. Add the flour and baking powder and thoroughly mix until combined into a thick dough. Slightly Knead on countertop to combine the ingredients thoroughly. (if needed)

3. On a well-floured surface use a rolling pin to roll ¼ of the dough then cut with a bone-shaped cookie cutter.

4. Evenly arrange on cookie sheet. Bake for approximately 18-20 minutes. Take a cookie sheet out of the oven and use a spatula to flip the cookies. Bake for an additional 10 more minutes until lightly browned.

5. Let cool before serving to your pup as a treat. Refrigerate or store at room temperature for a week.

Recipe 24: Stir Fry Beef Meal

This extremely simple stir fry is perfect for your dog, and you do not need a lot of ingredients to prepare it.

Makes: 5 cups

Total Prep Time: 25 mins.

Ingredient List:

- Ground beef (1 lb., lean)
- Pasta (whole wheat, small handful)
- Broccoli (1 cup, chopped)
- Carrots (4-5 medium sized, chopped)
- Water (2 cups)

HHHHHHHHHHHHHHHHHHHHHHHHHHHHHHHHHH

Instructions:

1. Add the beef, carrots, broccoli and water to a saucepan and bring to a boil.

2. Add the pasta and let simmer for approximately twenty minutes.

3. Cool before serving.

Recipe 25: Basic Dog Biscuits

These biscuits can be fashioned to suit your dog's desires.

Makes: 6

Total Prep Time: 40 mins.

Ingredient List:

- Egg (1)
- Flour (2 cups, whole wheat which is great for dogs that can consume to oats or white flour)
- Water (½ cup, hot)
- Salt (½ teaspoons)
- Chicken bouillon powder (1 teaspoon)
- There are other, ingredients (optional) that can be added, which includes liver powder, cheese (shredded), eggs, chicken / bacon.

HHHHHHHHHHHHHHHHHHHHHHHHHHHHHHHH

Instructions:

1. Preheat oven to 350 degrees Fahrenheit.

2. Dissolve bouillon in hot water and add the remaining ingredients.

3. Knead the dough for approximately 3 minutes until a ball has formed. Roll the dough to a thickness of ½ inch. Cut the dough with a bone-shaped cookie cutter.

4. Grease a cookie sheet lightly and place cookies on it.

5. Let bake for a minimum of 30 minutes.

Recipe 26: Doggie Meatballs

This is a fantastic recipe for older dogs who may find eating at times troublesome, as the meatballs are easy to consume. The pumpkin is one of nature's stool softeners, which is ideal for older dogs.

Makes: 12 cups

Total Prep Time: 30 mins.

Ingredient List:

- Beef (5 lb., ground)
- Oat bran (1 cup)
- Pumpkin puree (1 ½ cups)
- Carrots (2 large, mashed and boiled)
- kale (2 leaves, finely chopped)
- Bread (1 slice broken into small pieces)
- Eggs (2)
- Olive oil (for cookie sheets)

HHHHHHHHHHHHHHHHHHHHHHHHHHHHHHHHHH

Instructions:

1. Preheat oven to 350 degrees Fahrenheit.

2. In a large bowl place all the ingredients and use your hands to mix everything together and form into meatballs, the size of a doughnut hole.

3. Place the meatballs on the cookie sheets greased with olive oil, evenly spaced Ensuring not to place too closely together.

4. Use the olive oil to spray the meatballs if you prefer a caramelized look.

5. Bake in the oven for a minimum of 25 minutes or until it is thoroughly cooked.

6. Let cool. Divide into Ziploc bags in accordance of the dog's daily portion needs.

7. Let thaw before serving.

Recipe 27: Frozen Peanut Butter Yogurt Dog Treats

This easily prepared meal is perfect for when your dog needs to cool down after long intense play.

Makes: 12

Total Prep Time: 2 hrs.

Ingredient List:

- Peanut butter (1 cup)
- Vanilla yogurt (32 oz)

HHHHHHHHHHHHHHHHHHHHHHHHHHHHHHHHHH

Instructions:

1. Use a microwave-safe bowl to melt the peanut butter.

2. Mix yogurt with the melted peanut butter.

3. Pour mixture into paper cupcake liner. Store the filled cupcake liners in freezer.

Recipe 28: Salmon and Spinach

Here is a delicious recipe that will provide your pup with healthy fats and necessary carbs.

Makes: 1½ cups

Total Prep Time: 15 mins.

Ingredient List:

- Salmon (½ can, 3 oz, boneless, skinless and drained)
- Extra virgin olive oil (1 tablespoon)
- Spinach (½ cup, frozen, drained, chopped, and thawed)
- Eggs (2)

HHHHHHHHHHHHHHHHHHHHHHHHHHHHHHHHHH

Instructions:

1. Over medium heat, heat olive oil in a skillet.

2. Add the salmon and spinach, cooking until fully heated.

3. Add your egg and continue to cook until it's ready, which will take approximately two minutes.

4. Serve once cooled.

Recipe 29: Quinoa Doddie Plate

This meal is replenishing and great for your dog's diet if done in the correct manner. Quinoa is a great way to open your pet's diet to healthy grains.

Makes: 3-4

Total Prep Time: 35-40 mins.

Ingredient List:

- Water (4 cups)
- Olive oil (2 tablespoons)
- Quinoa (2 cups)
- Sweet potatoes (2 large)
- Sweet peas (2 cups)

HHHHHHHHHHHHHHHHHHHHHHHHHHHHHHHHHH

Instructions:

1. Add the quinoa and water in a saucepan and bring to a boil. Reduce the heat, cover, and simmer for approximately 15-20 minutes until quinoa becomes tender. Once finished, set aside.

2. Peel the sweet potatoes and microwave for a minimum of 10 minutes. Dice the potatoes.

3. Over medium heat, heat olive oil in a skillet and add the potatoes and sweet peas. Cook for an additional 10 more minutes.

4. Let the quinoa cool and combine with the sweet potatoes.

5. Serve warm. Refrigerate leftovers in fridge.

Recipe 30: Easy Chicken Stew

This is another really simple recipe that provides all of the nutrition your dog could need.

Makes: 6 cups

Total Prep Time: 40 mins.

Ingredient List:

- Chicken chunks (2 cups)
- Celery (2-3 sticks)
- Carrots (2 medium)
- Rice (1 cup, brown)
- kale (3-4 leaves)
- Water (2 cups)

HHHHHHHHHHHHHHHHHHHHHHHHHHHHHHHHHHH

Instructions:

1. Chop the vegetables.

2. In a suitable sized pot place the chicken chunks with carrots, chopped celery, and kale.

3. Add the brown rice and water and bring to boil. Reduce the heat to low. Cover and cook for a minimum of 30 minutes until the brown rice is finished.

4. Serve once cooled. Refrigerate any leftovers.

About the Author

Angel Burns learned to cook when she worked in the local seafood restaurant near her home in Hyannis Port in Massachusetts as a teenager. The head chef took Angel under his wing and taught the young woman the tricks of the trade for cooking seafood. The skills she had learned at a young age helped her get accepted into Boston University's Culinary Program where she also minored in business administration.

Summers off from school meant working at the same restaurant but when Angel's mentor and friend retired as head chef, she took over after graduation and created classic and new dishes that delighted the diners. The restaurant flourished under Angel's culinary creativity and one customer developed more than an appreciation for Angel's food. Several months after taking over the position, the young woman met her future husband at work and they have been inseparable ever since. They still live in Hyannis Port with their two children and a cocker spaniel named Buddy.

Angel Burns turned her passion for cooking and her business acumen into a thriving e-book business. She has authored several successful books on cooking different types of dishes using simple ingredients for novices and experienced chefs alike. She is still head chef in Hyannis Port and says she will probably never leave!

Author's Afterthoughts

With so many books out there to choose from, I want to thank you for choosing this one and taking precious time out of your life to buy and read my work. Readers like you are the reason I take such passion in creating these books.

It is with gratitude and humility that I express how honored I am to become a part of your life and I hope that you take the same pleasure in reading this book as I did in writing it.

Can I ask one small favour? I ask that you write an honest and open review on Amazon of what you thought of the book. This will help other readers make an informed choice on whether to buy this book.

My sincerest thanks,

Angel Burns

If you want to be the first to know about news, new books, events and giveaways, subscribe to my newsletter by clicking the link below

https://angel-burns.gr8.com

or Scan QR-code